The Graduate's Name Here

TO:

FROM:

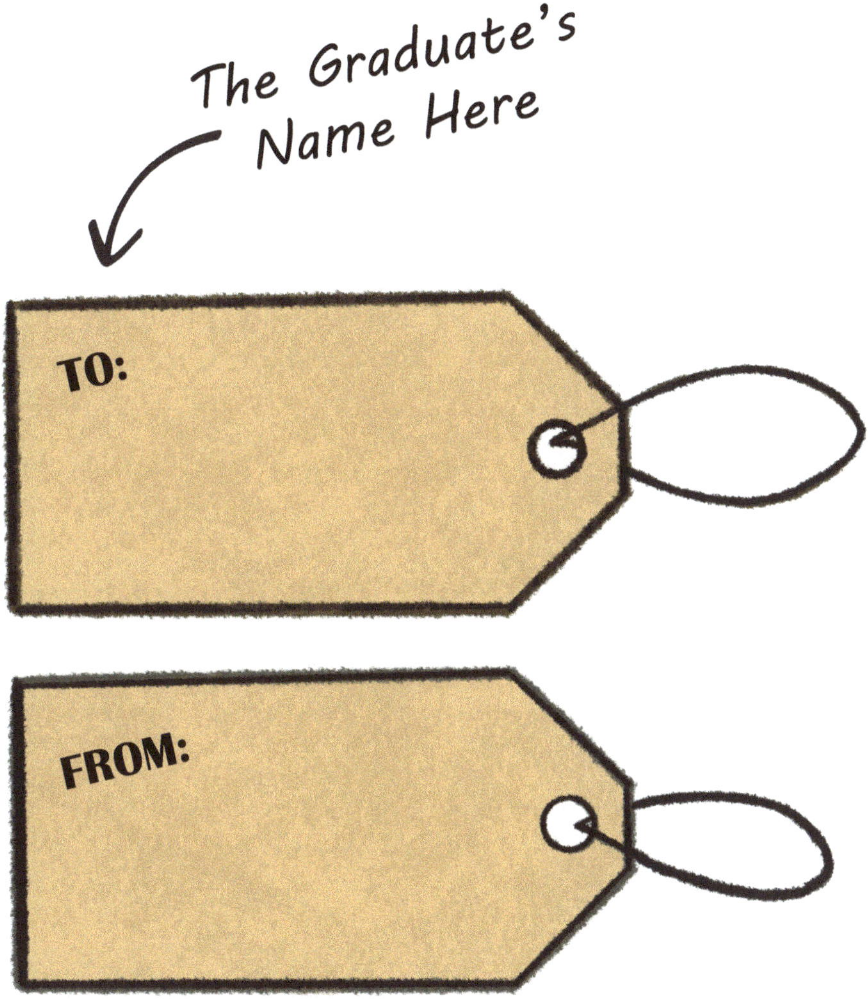

20 Minute Reads, LLC

To my sweetest sweets ~ Steve, Jack, Hudson & Remi - you all have my heart.

To my cousins - Andrea & Laurie.

To Derek for reading my stuff.

Thank you to my talented and helpful critique partners;

The Wild Things and The TUMS.

And my momma. Always my sweet momma.

And to all the graduates I'm so proud of...

Evan, Nick, Jordan,
Will, Jake, Carter,
Katherine, Sarah, Mark, Max, Tripp,
Laci, Casey, Caleb, Faith, Destiny, Alexis, Brett,
Kira, Faye, Sasha, Tage, Jackson, Emily, Emma, Payton,
Kyra, Sophia, Sevyn,
all the future graduates,
and my favorite 2023 grads...

Jack & Kyla!

You've got this!

Cassi

YOU DID IT!

Be Proud Of What You've Accomplished!

Things To Remember Now That You've Graduated!

Notice your blessings and be thankful.

There's always something to be grateful for.

"Acknowledging the good that you already have in your life is the foundation for all abundance."
~ Eckhart Tolle

*Need ideas? Turn to the back of the book.

Find your passion.
Find your purpose.

Pay attention to what you do in your spare time...

And do that!

*"The only way to do great work
is to love what you do."
~ Steve Jobs*

Believe in your dreams.

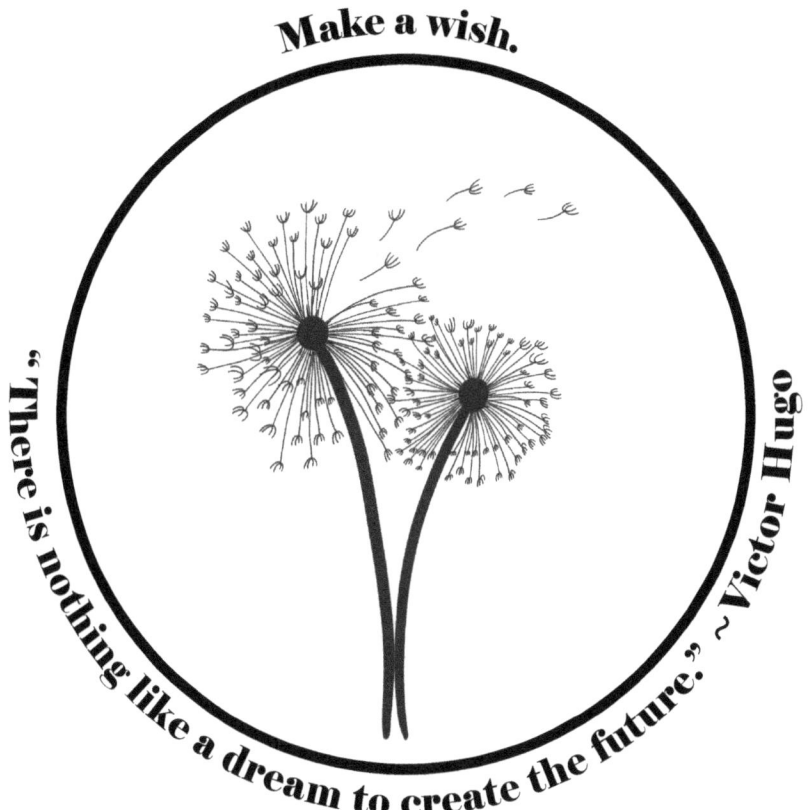

Make a wish.

"There is nothing like a dream to create the future." ~ Victor Hugo

"Never give up on what you really want to do.
The person with big dreams is more powerful
than the person with all the facts."
~ Albert Einstein

Be the best version of you!

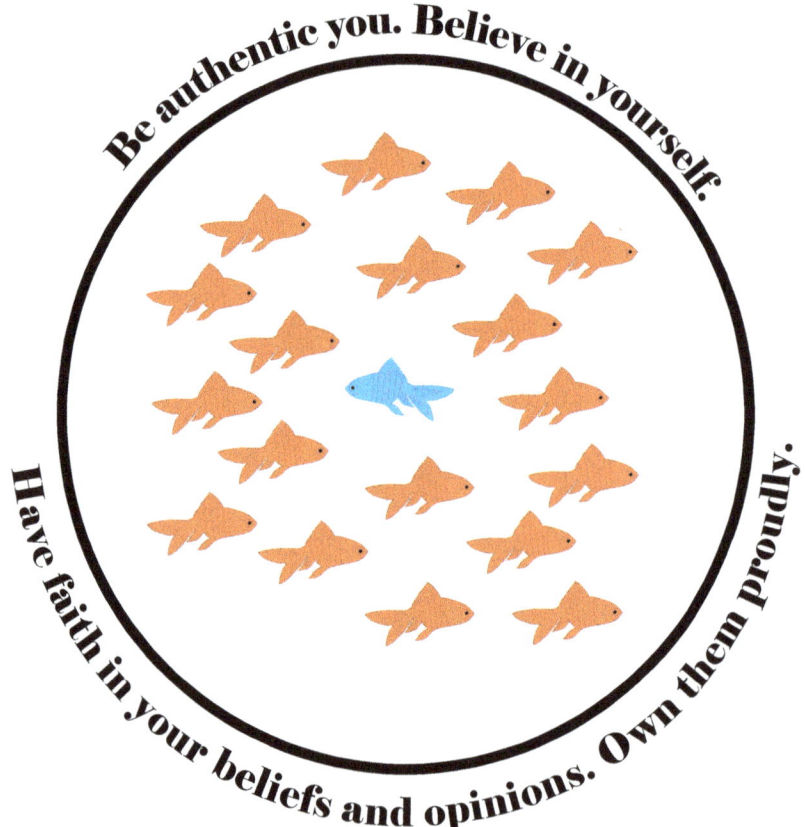

Be authentic you. Believe in yourself.
Have faith in your beliefs and opinions. Own them proudly.

"The opposite for courage is not cowardice,
it is conformity.
Even a dead fish can go with the flow."
~ Jim Hightower

Always be growing.

Read • Study • Observe • Learn

"Education breeds confidence.
Confidence breeds hope.
Hope breeds peace."
- Confucious

Find your happy.

*""The most important thing is to enjoy your life
- to be happy - it's all that matters."
~ Audrey Hepburn*

Take risks and try new things.

Discover who you are.

"Do one thing every day that scares you." ~ Eleanor Roosevelt

"And the day came
when the risk to remain tight in a bud
was more painful than the risk it took to blossom."
~ Anais Nin

But be mindful and safe.

Lock your doors. Be aware of your surroundings.

Be safe.

Never leave your drink unattended.

Listen to your gut and trust it.
Even if it's just a whisper.

Read The Gift of Fear by Gavin de Becker

Find confidence.

Stand tall • shoulders back • Head held high

Take up space. Make yourself big.

"Show up in every single moment like you're meant to be there."
~ Marie Forleo

Be open to love and friendship but don't compromise who you are for anyone, ever.

"Love all, trust a few." ~ William Shakespeare

"Friendship is a single soul dwelling in two bodies."
~ Aristotle

Ask for help if you need it.

Talk to your parents, a friend, a counselor. #988

Asking for help is a sign of strength.

"Don't be afraid to ask questions.
Don't be afraid to ask for help when you need it."
~ President Barack Obama

Be kind.

Be kind to others - you never know what people are going through. And don't listen to the bully in your head. Be nice to you.

"Be kind whenever possible.
It's always possible."
~ Dalai Lama

Don't compare yourself to others.

We're all on our own journey.

"Be yourself;
everyone else is already taken."
~ Oscar Wilde

Be helpful.
Doing for others brings
the purist happiness.

Open doors • pay it forward • your kindness makes a difference.

*"The art of being helpful is behaving
as if everything we do matters -
because we never know which things might."
-Gloria Steinem*

Have some manners!

Napkin in your lap • sit up straight • always thank the cook • don't start eating until everyone is seated• Say please & thank you•

"Good manners reflect something from inside –
an innate sense of consideration for others
and respect for self."
~ Emily Post

Be a good listener.

Talk less, hear more.

"The quieter you become,
the more you are able to hear."
~ Rumi

Set clear boundaries.

"A lack of boundaries invites a lack of respect." ~ Ritu Ghatourey

"Be careful what you tolerate.
You are teaching people how to treat you."
~ Unknown

Learn the art of small talk.

"The art of conversation lies in the listening."
~Malcolm S. Forbes

Be honest with yourself and others.

Truth - it makes life easier.

"If you tell the truth, you don't have to remember anything." ~ Mark Twain

"Three things cannot be long hidden: the sun, the moon, and the truth."
~ Buddha

Create good habits.

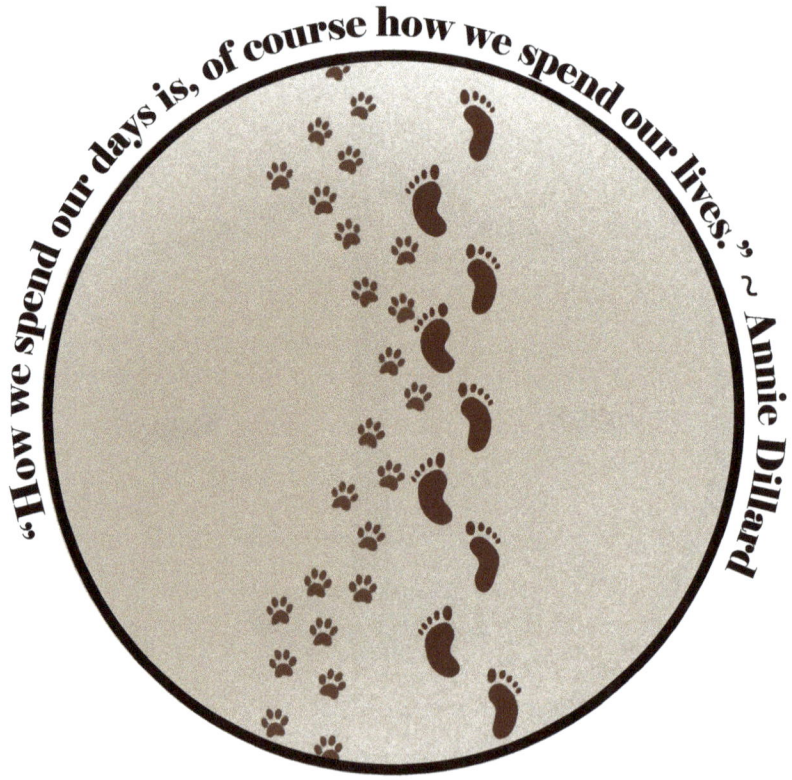

"How we spend our days is, of course how we spend our lives." ~ Annie Dillard

"People do not decide their futures,
they decide their habits
and their habits decide their futures."
~F. Matthias Alexander

Move your body every day.

Exercise gives you energy.

Work up a sweat everyday.

"A body in motion tends to stay in motion."
~ Isaac Newton, First Laws of Motion

Get in the sun!

The sun is life's happy vitamin.

Take care of your skin- wear sunscreen and moisturizer.

"Keep your face always toward the sunshine
and shadows will fall behind you.'
~ Walt Whitman

Don't forget to play!
And dance and sing and paint.
Create every chance you get.

But also let yourself get quiet - that's when the ideas come in.

"The world always seems brighter when you've just made something that wasn't there before."

~ Neil Gaiman

Get out in nature as much as you can.

Surround yourself with fresh air.

And just breathe.

"Of all the paths you take in life, make sure a few of them are dirt."
~ John Muir

Stop Procrastinating,
But Don't Expect Perfection.

"Slow and Steady Wins The Race"

The Tortoise & The Hare

"The best is the mortal enemy of the good."
~Voltaire

Be mindful of money.

"A penny saved is a penny earned."
~ Benjamin Franklin

Drink your water.

Our bodies are made up of 55-60% water. *

"Hydrate!" ~ Archie Mountbatten-Windsor

"Water is the driving force of all nature."
~ Leonardo da Vinci

*According to the US Geological Survey.
(usga.gov)

Make sure you get good, quality sleep.

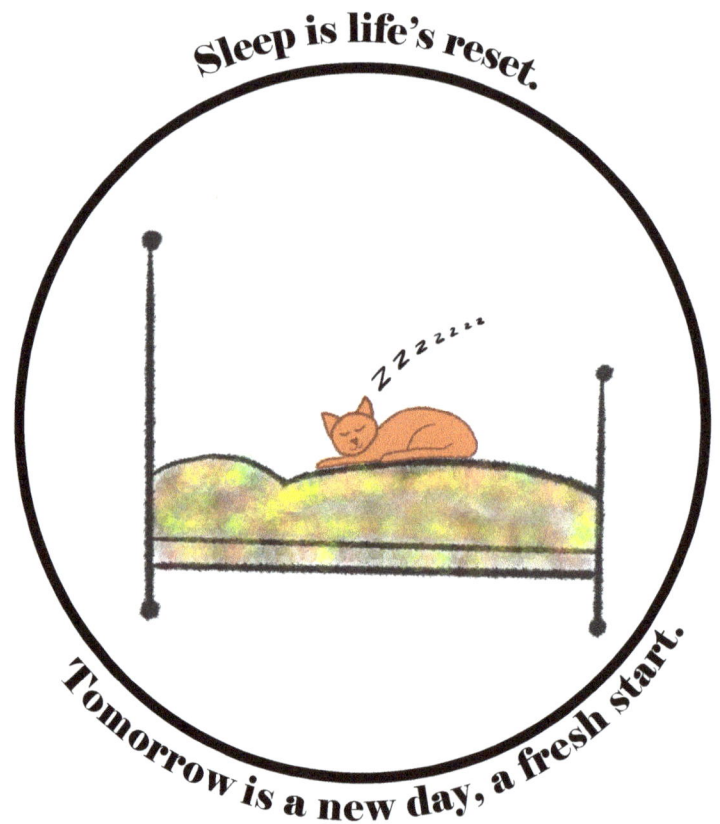

Sleep is life's reset.

Z z z z z z z

Tomorrow is a new day, a fresh start.

*"Almost everything will work again
if you unplug it for a few minutes - including you."
~Anne Lamott*

Eat your fruits and veggies.

You'll feel better.

*"Let food be thy medicine
and medicine be thy food."
~ Hippocrates*

Take care of your teeth.

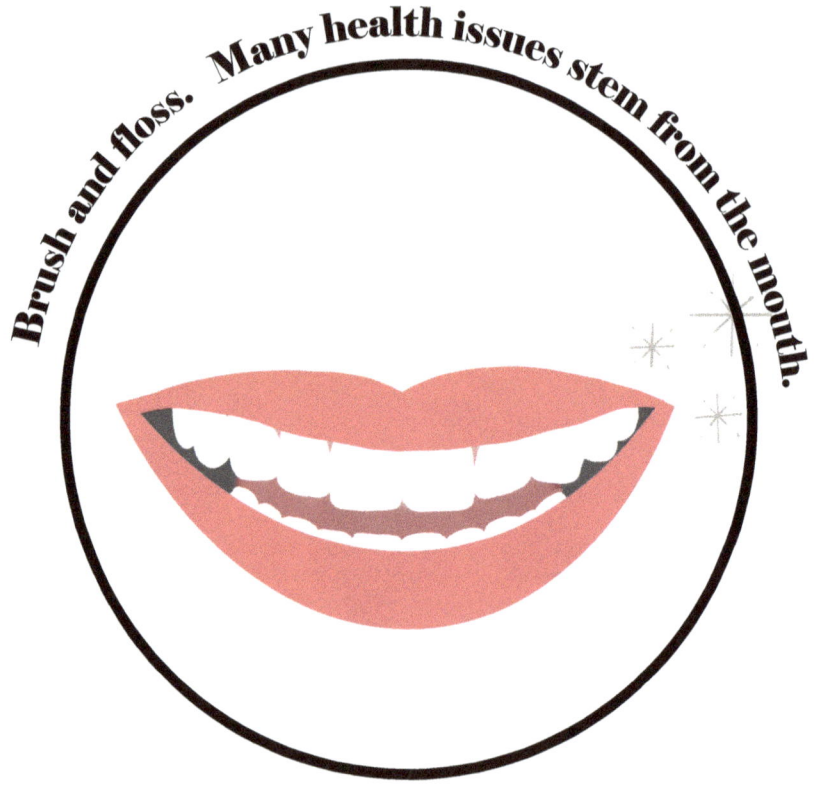

Brush and floss. Many health issues stem from the mouth.

Replace your toothbrush every three months.
~ every dentist ever

Be a good driver.

With 4,000 pounds of power comes great responsibility.

Don't get in the car with anyone under the influence.
(alcohol, drugs, lack of sleep, etc.)

Take a moment to enjoy the sunsets.

"There is nothing more musical than a sunset." ~ Claude Debussy

"Every sunset brings the promise of a new dawn."
~ Ralph Waldo Emerson

And then look up at the stars.

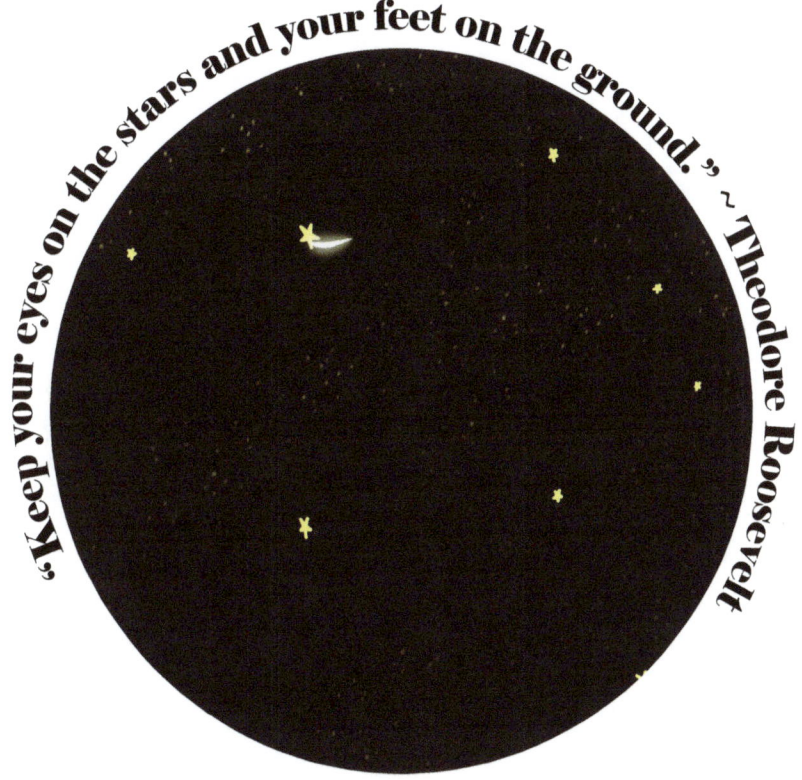

"Keep your eyes on the stars and your feet on the ground." ~ Theodore Roosevelt

"Remember to look up at the stars
and not down at your feet.
Try to make sense of what you see and wonder about
what makes the universe exist. Be curious."
~ Stephen Hawking

Adventure Awaits!

"You always have choices." ~ Janalee

"You can do anything you decide to do." ~Amelia Earhart

"If you don't like the road you're walking, start paving another one."
~ Dolly Parton

Thankful List

The cold side of the pillow
Morning coffee
Your best friend
A call from your mom
A cupcake
Puppy kisses
An awe inspiring sunset
A hot bath
Ice water on a hot day
A good belly laugh
New shoes
Finding $20 in your winter coat pocket
Kayaking on a river
Listening to the birds
A hug from a grandparent
A good dream
A job well done
A sense of accomplishment
A compliment
Doing something for others
Paying it forward
Family
Pizza
Mangoes
A good book
Sweet dreams
Hot chocolate with lots of whip cream
Toes in the sand at the beach
Looking at the ocean
Chocolate
Connecting with friends
A heartfelt hug
Going to the movies
Music

Notes & Stuff To Remember